WHAT'S THE POINT?

*Determine the point
of your work and daily life.*

Dani ✶

DANI GRIEVESON

Copyright 2023 © Dani Grieveson.

All Rights Reserved.

No part of this publication may be reproduced, distributed, or transmitted in any form or by any means, including photocopying, recording, or other electronic or mechanical methods, without the prior written permission of the publisher, except in the case of brief quotations embodied in critical reviews and certain other non-commercial uses permitted by copyright law.

TABLE OF CONTENTS

Introduction 1

Chapter 1: Clarity 9

Feel The Fire Inside…And Pursue That 11
Looking at Your Life…...14
Find Clarity By Finding What's Within YOU and Then Your Why 15

Clarity Power Questions 19

Chapter 2: Confidence 21

My Shattered Confidence That Had To Be Rebuilt 26
Choose Your Words — And Your Friends — Carefully 30
Find Your Top 5 Points And Activate Them 32

Challenging Your Inner Critic 37

Chapter 3: Focus & Discipline 39

To Avoid a Downward Spiral 47
Focus on YOUR Positive Points 47
Successful Self-Talk 47

Power questions for your better focus 49

Chapter 4: Routine 51

Energy Givers & Takers 53
Key Areas Of Focus In Your Routine 55

Protecting Your Energy..61
Power questions for your better routine......................................63

Chapter 5: Fulfilment 65
Finding Fulfilment In Your Life: The Starting Point 70
What Makes You Come Alive? 75
Power questions to find your fulfilment......................................78

Chapter 6: Success & Sustainability..79
'I Can Do Better Than This!' 83
Power questions to your success..87

Conclusion 89
About The Author..95
Praise of Dani Grieveson's work 97

Standing on this pontoon years ago at Chichester Marina, after much contemplation, I decided to passionately pursue the point of my life.

This photo is enlarged and framed in my bathroom to remind me (whilst I brush my teeth each day) to proactively live that point.

Let's dive into what your point is together.

INTRODUCTION

Greetings and a big bravo *to you* for making an effort *for you* towards a more confident, fulfilled and substantiated life.

Your life. It's your biggest and best calling, isn't it? But what is it about for you? What's the point of your life?

Increasingly, we become overwhelmed by career, health trends, relationships, finances, family and therefore how full life is, then we can become lost in what we're doing it all for.

If that resonates, please keep reading. If you're the kind of person who likes to wallow, your problems are your security blanket and you want to stay stuck, this book isn't for you.

If you're the kind of person who has challenges, sometimes feels lost and yet, you know there is more in this life for you, please read on.

If you answer 'yes' to any of the first eight questions below, and 'no' to the ninth, then you've found the right book:

1. Have you ever found yourself in a downward spiral?

2. Do you know there is more for you?

3. Have you felt unfulfilled?

4. Have you struggled with your confidence?

5. Do you understand what you're truly capable of?

6. Do you become consumed by negative beliefs and thoughts?

7. Have you experienced a trauma or tragedy and you know you need to get your life back on track?

8. Have you left a difficult job/relationship/family member and that's driving you to make a change?

9. Are you being all you were created to be?

Right now, it's time to stop losing yourself in life and change for the better. Does that sound good? If so, I've created this book for you, to help you discover and *live* the point of your life.

We all have a distinctive point to our life and there is no right or wrong. And from me, there's no judgment on what yours is. Moving through our journey together, please be free to explore, to examine, and to make a few wrong turns - as that's exactly how we grow.

Reading this book (as long as you stay with it), I promise you will help sharpen and strengthen who you are, and pinpoint for you what your life is about.

Through life, I have pondered those nine questions, like you just have dear reader and ardently searched for the greatest answers. Alongside fastidious research I have pursued and encounters with thousands of people from the slums of India to billionaires in Switzerland, I've designed six pillars for human development. These pillars help activate our human capacity to experience the full colour of our work and daily life.

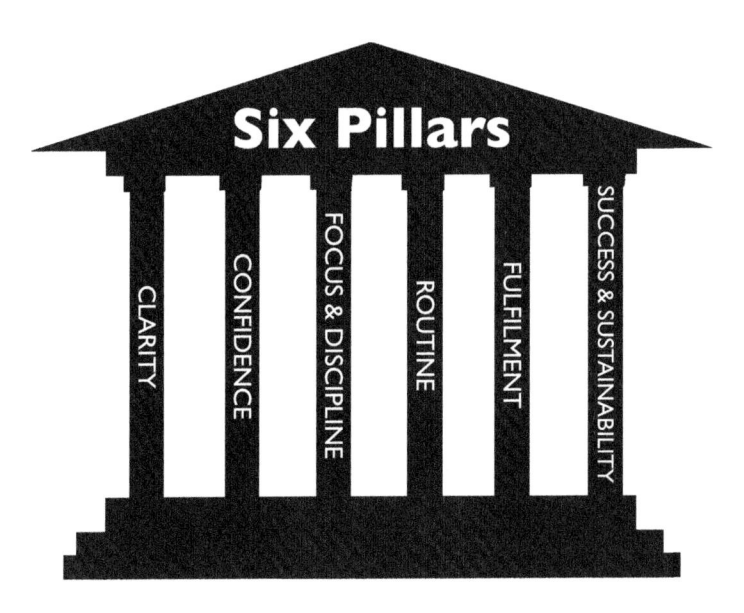

Six Pillars

- CLARITY
- CONFIDENCE
- FOCUS & DISCIPLINE
- ROUTINE
- FULFILMENT
- SUCCESS & SUSTAINABILITY

My name is Dani, and I lead a business called Lift This Life (you'll learn why it was called that within this book) but more than that, I'm a fighter, a woman who won't give up, who has failed so many times, been ignored, rejected and isolated more times than I want to recall. This has meant, *knowing* the point of my life, has kept me anchored, strong and passionate when I encounter life's punches. So, I've designed this book to align you with your point in life, so that when you experience a setback, you're stronger and sharper to come back.

I can help you do this because I've made many wrong turns, trusted, and invested in the wrong people, and found myself in traumatic situations which at times, took me down (the suicide of a close friend, being sexually abused and experiencing domestic violence to share just some of my lived setbacks with you).

My journey in human development started working in the slums of India back in 2002. In India I've worked with non-governmental organisations that support abandoned and abused children, drug-addicted street children and girls trafficked for sexual exploitation. I have a heart for those who are sexually violated, as you may now understand.

*Working in India, Jay Prakesh on my left, Pankaj on my right
– wonderful boys with huge hearts.*

From my work in India, to now in powerfully developing people in prisons to companies such as Deloitte, Bentley Motors to their next level through finding confidence and fulfilment (not just saccharine or "jazz hands" happiness). I want to share with you the learnings, tools and techniques for discovering and truly living the point of your life.

Here in "What's The Point?" I give you robust ways to strengthen your path in living a deeply contented and yet uplifted level of life.

Using my personal drive to experience all that life can be meant that, before I started my own business, I worked with The Olympic Games, Mercedes-Benz, the BBC, Top Gear, Coca-Cola, and Rolls-Royce Motor Cars. My mission while working for these brands was always to bring strength and success to the people and projects I've worked with. Undoubtedly, strength and success happen within people first.

Sir Clive Woodward said:

> "Sport is results through people.
> Business is results through people."

In bringing success within people and fulfilling my mission to live the point of my life in enabling others to truly know theirs, it's not been a straightforward process. Nothing is, sorry to say. This book has a meticulously researched six-pillar process to fortify you in discovering and unleashing the point of your life.

Now, I'm delighted to fully live the point of my life – which is to power people UP to their strength and success. The point, therefore, of my life distils to me putting my head on the pillow at night, knowing that others have breathed easier because of my existence.

Maybe that sounds simple? Like with many simple things in life, finding the point of your life requires learning - often through making mistakes - refining and dedication. This is precisely why I created this six-pillar framework to encourage others to maximise their experience of work and daily life through accomplishing their authentic goals and aspirations.

Whatever your success is – whatever the point of your life is – your success and why you're here are intrinsically linked. They're not juxtaposed because, surely, success *is* fully living the point of your life.

In her book, The Top Five Regrets of the Dying by palliative care nurse Bronnie Ware, she wrote that the number one regret of patients was:

> "I wish I'd had the courage to live a life true to myself, not the life others expected of me."

Consequently, let's start now, living a life of courage and being true to yourself.

Life can be tough, yes, it can. But you can be tough too and, together, we can make your life one of fulfilment, with a clear point for you.

So come on, let's get the point of your life shining, together.

Roman poet, Horace, in 23 BC wrote 'Carpe Diem'. Now that was over 2000 years ago, and this type of thinking is a springboard for how I navigate life.

We're here, now. Just this once. Therefore, we must make it a sensational life, I hope you're the kind of person who agrees with that.

If you're not, that's okay, but then this clearly isn't the book for you. For my Carpe Diem tribe, please read on.

I don't profess to have all the answers, but I certainly have some valuable tools for you in the upcoming chapters.

Over the last 2000 years, thinkers, philosophers, psychologists and leaders haven't discovered the holy grail in life and humbly, I acknowledge I haven't either, but I am going to help you to stop searching, to stop spiralling downwards, and finally find YOUR point to life.

The real, authentic you.

So, in this book, I'm going to show you how to:

- Find clarity in your life
- Develop your confidence
- Focus
- Find an energising routine
- Discover greater fulfilment
- Realise *your* success – for work and daily life

Thank you for choosing to improve your life with me and taking time to discover yourself. This book is designed to demonstrate to you how to fully live the point of your life.

I am looking forward to sharing the greatest of what I've learnt with you.

Are you ready? Seatbelt fastened? Tray table up?

Let's take off together.

Chapter 1

CLARITY

"Do what you feel in your heart to be right – for you'll be criticized anyway."

Eleanor Roosevelt

University is supposed to be the time when we set foundations for a career path…and have some fun at student parties along the way.

Here, it felt like the foundations of my life were crumbling. Within three months of my first year at Oxford Brookes University in England I knew I'd made a huge mistake.

"What am I doing here?"

"This just doesn't feel right."

"What is it that I actually want to do for the rest of my life?"

Just some of the feelings frequenting my extremely busy and undeveloped 19-year-old brain as I tried to find a clear direction forward. But I was truly lost, confused… and hadn't eaten for five days straight.

I just didn't enjoy or connect with the course that I was on. Having studied and gone to lectures for those first three months, as well as having made new friends and been to a plethora of student nights out, my life and my future just weren't fitting together or feeling good.

What could my future hold? Would I still feel lost after university? I was in a place where I didn't like myself as a result of this wrong educational choice. I'd made a terrible mistake and I couldn't see the bigger picture.

Nothing was making any sense to me. And then there was the heavy pressure that I'd do well because of the circumstances I'd been brought up in.

I became so low and lost with it all that an eating disorder I'd previously had at school resurfaced. I'd had anorexia at school which developed to combine with horrible bulimia (horrible because physically making yourself sick, time and time again is an awful process for the body and mind…) and going without food, or making myself vomit, became the norm because I simply felt so low, confused and uncertain.

This was the rest of my life I was trying to create, and I couldn't see any clear path forward for myself.

Zero clarity.

Plenty of confusion.

How could I get back on track and find a way forward out of the mess?

Feel The Fire Inside…And Pursue That

I was determined to complete the degree, but I simply couldn't face several more years of nothing but university life. Despite that extremely rocky first year as a student, the extreme lows taught me a valuable lesson: **to pursue what you love.**

"Dani, you've got to sort this out," I thought to myself. The option of NOT sorting my life out wasn't so appealing. I wanted to get out into the working world, and I also wanted to do something that would light life up.

My degree was obviously not fulfilling me – in fact it was depressing me and really bringing me down – so I had to intentionally discover what would fulfil me and what would create joy for myself and others in this life.

At school, I'd loved studying drama (I'm still in touch with our marvellous drama teacher, Mrs Fisher, today). I relished the theory of drama and the academic basis of learning, such as discovering Brechtian techniques or the directing process of Stanislavski. However, in school drama lessons, I'd never looked at the behind-the-scenes production or applying the theory – the drama course was fantastic and yet a lot of what we did was realised on stage. Now, I wanted to get under the skin of production, to make it happen, to be behind the scenes making the performance exceptional.

And so, in my second year of university, I rallied the troops on the course and around the wider university community and directed a production of Grease The Musical. It sold out every night and received standing ovations. It felt fantastic to do this. I met a variety of people, made great connections, flexed behind-the-scenes production muscles I'd never known about, and started feeling alive doing what I love. I felt I wasn't born to take centre stage; I was born to support others to do that for their lives. This experience gave me clarity – and pointed me in the right direction for my next steps.

Behind-the-scenes production captivated me. I found work experience at a radio station around my degree, and then in my third year, I started work experience on Top Gear at the BBC. That perplexing and difficult first year at university was left behind me and the eating disorder had thankfully resolved – I was embracing life and what brought me alive.

It was clear why my health was restored, and my enthusiasm had returned: because I decided to pursue what lit me up, on the inside. I now see that it's vital to discover what sets a fire alive inside of you... and then follow that path.

I believe as long as we're not hurting ourselves or those around us, we MUST actively pursue what brings us ALIVE.

We put enormous pressure on ourselves to figure everything out, to know who we are and what we must do, at a young age. I know I certainly did. Whilst unstimulated by my degree, it spring boarded me into finding work experience in radio and television. Now in my working life, I'm pleased take on work experience students from universities, to help them explore what they like and don't like in the working world.

Additionally, I know it helps boost their CV for their future career path. My work experience did and I'm very grateful for that. Plus, I'm delighted to give a great reference when they do a brilliant job. Some of my work experience students have gone on to work in journalism, tech and automotive.

When I interview students, I always say: "It is okay if you don't know what you want to do right now. It's okay."

At first, I felt confined in that university environment and didn't feel I could explore my passions or discover other avenues. In those days, I felt I had to do just one thing with my future. I felt both trapped and lost at the same time.

Looking at Your Life...

Could you imagine driving and no road signs marked on the road? You'd have no idea where you'd been, where you are, or where you are going to be.

Your life is pretty similar. You need a clear roadmap to help you navigate the twists and turns, plus know the vital points you want to get to along the way.

Leadership expert, John Maxwell, said, "Clarity of vision, expresses clarity of priorities."

Like me, have you ever felt completely lost?

Is your work environment suffocating you, but you need the finances?

Has your relationship just become comfortable and not romantic or exciting for you?

Are you feeling more confused than clear?

Is your life spiralling into chaos?

Do you feel conflict within yourself and often with others?

Have you been struggling to make good decisions?

Are you feeling like just giving up in your relationship, at work, in your health, in your motivation?

Are you frequently doubting yourself?

Have you found yourself quite forgetful because of your confusion?

Do you know you're not taking necessary action?

Let us stop that downward spiral.

Find Clarity By Finding What's Within YOU and Then Your Why

> *"What lies behind us, and what lies before us are tiny matters compared to what lies within us."*
>
> Ralph Waldo Emerson, *philosopher*

What's within YOU, is yours. There are tiny miracles inside you. Whether you're a great communicator, an empath, a competitor, a natural analyser of information, super with numbers, a strong problem solver or brilliant with people you'll know what you're naturally best and brilliant at.

There are and have been many notable people in the world, for example, Florence Nightingale, Winston Churchill, Steve Jobs, Alan Turing, Oprah Winfrey, Ruth Bader Ginsburg, Martin Luther King Jr, Beyoncé, and Nelson Mandela – each of these people understood what made them different and use it – to their global success and making our history books.

You must discover what the miracles within you are and crucially, you have to *use* what's within you. You must act.

What's within you is yours. Your point in life is distinctive.

How are you applying your miracles within to your work or daily life? Or are you?

Do you understand what is within you?

Your potential is UNIQUE. Just like Beyoncé's or Nelson Mandela's - as the great poet Mary Oliver said, "Tell me, what are you going to do with your one, wild and precious life."

In unravelling your wild and precious life and get some all-important clarity in your life, let's begin our journey together.

> **"Have the courage to follow your heart and intuition. They somehow know what you truly want to become."**
>
> Steve Jobs

When I start working with people, I usually ask them to define their success. Success is very different from person to person. Society says success is wealth, fame, and likes on social media – but not many people I work with have said that's what their vision for success looks like.

What's yours?

We've all heard of Donald Trump and Mother Theresa, haven't we? Donald Trump, it feels to me that his vision for success is almighty power. Whereas Mother Theresa, her vision for success was almighty service to the poor. Both are very effective people in pursuing their vision for success.

Come on then, let's get you clearer and more effective.

1. Define your success – clarity of this is your superpower in life. It will keep you anchored and strong in challenging times. Try as I might through this book and my work, we're never going to stop the challenging times. Just as you'll laugh in life, you'll cry – and you need a strong anchor for those moments. So find your clarity – ask yourself what your success is and vitally *why* do you want this?

2. Now, let's move you to pursuing that effectively. Claim your mindset, find focus and energy.

3. Next, take action towards your success, and replace bad habits you have (more to come in the "routine" section on this). What do you need to do today to get you there? Dreams don't come true unless you pursue them.

4. Study others' success. Who can you model yourself on? Who has done something similar? What did they do? What did they not do?

Your power is in execution. What three small steps can you make today towards your vision for success? I say small because the bigger and more overwhelming those steps are, the less likely you are to start *fully living* the point of your life.

Remember that complexity creates complication in execution. And in executing (acting), is where your power lies.

Keep your plan, the point, and your life simple.

CLARITY POWER QUESTIONS

1. What made you show interest in this book?

2. How do you define your vision for work?

3. What does a great day look like?

4. Who are you?

5. How do you think?

6. What does your wiser self know – that you pretend not to, or would rather avoid?

7. Who do you admire?

8. Who do you follow online?

9. Who would you never dream of following?

10. Who do you dislike?

11. What type of books do you read?

12. What type of books do you never read?

Chapter 2

CONFIDENCE

You cannot have a bright life, a vibrant life, or live fully, without confidence. I'm very serious about this because a lack of confidence can cause a host of major problems in life for you. I truly believe that when you don't have confidence, you're not living your life.

Low confidence impacts your quality of life, and not for the better. You can see a downward trend in so many areas, your sleep, your stress, your diet, your performance at work, and your kindness to your family and friends. Negative feelings about yourself and self-criticism can develop into feelings of sadness, depression, anxiety, anger, shame, fear or guilt. Which I don't want for you.

Here are some indicators that you have low confidence:

- Losing control or needing to control
- Negative social comparisons
- Trouble asking for help
- Worry and doubt

- Difficulty accepting compliments
- Harsh self-talk
- Fear of failure
- A negative outlook for your future
- Lacking personal boundaries
- People pleasing
- Dwelling on defeats

If you see any of these indicators in yourself, you're reading the right book. Thank you for being part of this journey, trust me, it's not an easy one to finding confidence but it's a great one when it comes together.

When your confidence is low, or worse lost, mistakes happen. You don't know who you are, what you value, the credibility that you bring to work and daily life. You are unclear on your own identity. It's easy to trust the wrong people or projects because you don't have an in-built belief or value system within yourself.

And so, when people say things to you (individuals who have their own agenda and/or greater confidence than you), they may use words that can be comforting, and it's easy to become influenced by that. And that comforting language we hear from other people is affirming you… when you can't affirm yourself.

This is really important, certainly when we look at romantic relationships. We often hear that people get into relationships – and they lose their identity. They give so much of themselves away, and their confidence becomes so low that they eventually don't recognize who they are. I speak from experience…and I know of many, many other cases where this has occurred.

Equally in career situations, when confidence is low, it's easy to get directed into a role or tasks that we don't necessarily want. One that suits the business but doesn't suit your strength. From a place of low confidence, we can be moulded into what suits other people's needs rather than optimising our value and strength.

When I look at caregivers who support other people, they may not necessarily be low in confidence, but when one pours into other people so much, it's easy to lose oneself. Similarly, if we look at the NHS in England, we have a staffing crisis, with high turnover, burn out and we cannot recruit enough medics. With pay disputes, strikes, and not enough resources, the NHS as an organisation and culture is struggling.

Without proper strengthening and support, when people care so much for other people, it can lead to stress and burnt-out.

In his book, Burn Out, Herbert Freudenberger describes the three components of Burn Out:

1. Emotional exhaustion — the fatigue that comes from caring too much for too long.

2. Depersonalisation — the depletion that comes from empathy, caring and compassion.

3. Decreased sense of accomplishment — the unconquerable sense of futility, feeling that nothing you do makes any difference

People who pour energy and focus into other people and are not having their energy filled back up means they can end up feeling depleted, questioning the difference they make, and thus affecting their confidence.

I see this in many organisations that I work with. The high expectations within teams and to deliver the results can lead to burn out, costing the business money in recruitment fees and/or staff sickness. That's why, these days, I love delivering high performance without burn out programmes.

To avoid low confidence or burn out it's critical to understand what makes you, you. To know your identity and to acknowledge the value that you bring to work and daily life. Recognising *the value inside yourself* is vital for a healthy and happy life for you. Not the value of the car you drive, the holidays you go on or the clothes you wear, all of this is external validation – when your power comes from knowing what is within you.

Tal Ben-Shahar, a former Harvard professor who taught the most popular course at Harvard, 'positive psychology', discusses in his book 'Happier' the concept of 'emotional bankruptcy' at a time when we have more material wealth than ever. Yet we have the biggest mental health crisis of all time. Personally, I want to keep you emotionally healthy, not emotionally bankrupt, and you need to know what's right with you to do just that.

Revered psychologist Carl Jung said: "The least of things with a meaning is worth more in life that the greatest of things without it."

I want to help you find meaning, fulfilment, and richness to your life so that your life is one with a point; a life of meaning.

To build this, it's vital to ensure you maintain your own level of self-care. Self-care is essentially what makes you, you. I've worked with a variety of people to help them understand what self-care is to them and crucially do it. Everyone is different in what self-care looks like to them. It can be writing poetry, connecting with loved ones, taking time in nature and one chap found that a daily wrestle with his dog made him feel at his best! Whatever works for you to build you UP (so long as you're not hurting yourself or others) is your self-care.

When we don't have confidence, we can find ourselves pouring into that other person's emotional pot and not filling our pot up, which is unhealthy. And when our confidence is low and we're not in control of our emotions, we can find ourselves in a self-destruct mode. It may be drinking too much. It may be comfort eating. It could be taking drugs or forming unhealthy habits and/or relationships.

And then, of course, another extreme of not being in control of emotions such as anger, fear and low confidence is that people commit crimes and end up in prison. This year I've been holding workshops in prisons, speaking to inmates about developing their self-confidence. This has been extremely valuable work because I feel extremely passionate about focusing on confidence as a core foundational pillar for people.

> When we feel confident,
> we are clear on the value we bring.
> We are clear on what's positive about us.
> More importantly, we behave
> in accordance with our personal
> positive points.

And when we act upon what's right about us, our life is brighter, more vibrant, and much more fulfilled. That's where I really want to get people to because when you don't have your true confidence, you are not authentically living your life.

My Shattered Confidence That Had To Be Rebuilt

Nowadays, I empower people on their self-confidence at meetings, seminars, conferences, workshops, and in everyday one-on-one conversations. I can develop people in confidence very confidently! But it wasn't always this way. In fact, my confidence was broken several years ago, having been chipped away bit by bit in an unhealthy relationship.

I was betrayed by a partner. I discovered he was secretly seeing other women. I just knew there was something wrong because of the incredibly dismissive way he was behaving towards me, and I'm not shy to admit that to reason with my gut feeling, I read his social media messages.

There were three different women that I discovered he was 'entertaining' around the world, and I confronted him.

"I know there are more women than just me in this relationship," I said to him. He just looked at me blankly for a second or two before firing back at me, "What are you talking about? I'm sick of this. I'm sick of you. You're nothing but a psycho!"

I'd seen those messages in black and white. I know what I'd read. I'd discovered what was really going on. Yet somehow, because I held him on such a pedestal and had given so much of myself into our relationship, I actually believed him. I thought to myself, "Yes, it's my fault, I've got it wrong. I must be a psycho."

I took those words and carried them with me for years. Over time, I felt there was so much wrong with me, and that I had no value, and I was not worth loving. And, at that time, I was working every day in an environment where none of my experience or positive points were recognised or valued. My desk was opposite a director's office door, that I was consistently shut out of. Day after day, week after week, month after month, year after year.

The company directors often undermined me publicly, time and time again, giving me the most mundane and basic jobs, such as stapling, organising paperwork, and printing. Now, I'm really not averse to hard work. Of course, not…but the admin team were available next to me.

I felt that this was a way of humiliating me, undermining my value by giving me mundane and simple tasks when I had so much more to offer. One day a colleague said to me, "You're wasted here Dani" but I'd lost so much belief in myself, I didn't feel I had much value in work or daily life.

This began to dishearten me, at work and in daily life – I was crestfallen. Being betrayed by my partner, not being "good enough" for him – and then blamed for the problems he was causing "you're a psycho." Compounded by working in a suppressing environment where I was shut out day after day after day, month after month, it affected my mindset and shattered my confidence. I found myself in a place of not knowing my worth or value. And I believed it, I simply didn't feel good enough, for anything or anybody.

I honestly got into the car leaving work on so many evenings thinking that I was on the scrapheap of life. In my mind I'd think, 'I can't be living this life any longer, this can't be my life', but that's how it continued day after day. Then to really shine a spotlight on those negative thoughts and self-beliefs, I had my first big meeting in work. I was to organise the meeting for the whole business and handled it as professionally as possible.

One person was 20 minutes late for the meeting, and none of the others wanted to start without this person. After this inaugural meeting to showcase what I'd worked on, I politely asked for a quick chat, and asked: "Can you please let me know why you were late? No one wanted to start without you being there, so it was a bit of an awkward start to the meeting. Can you just let me know why?"

And this person replied: "I think your meeting lacked structure."

I was a little taken aback and said: "It's a response I can take and yet I have organised meetings previously with other organisations such as Coca-Cola Rolls-Royce and the BBC, and…"

"EVERYTHING ABOUT YOU AND YOUR EXPERIENCE MEANS F*CK ALL!" she bluntly said in my face before I even got to finish the sentence.

It was cruel. It was tough to take it. And those words hurt at a time when I was already hurting badly. She obviously didn't realise what was going on in my personal life, or my mental state at that point, but this can hold true in many situations in our everyday life.

Choose Your Words —
And Your Friends — Carefully.

We have to be very cautious about the words that we choose to say to people. So, when we're looking at building confidence and strength in ourselves and around ourselves, look at the people you are surrounding yourself with – and be discerning.

> ***"You're the average of the five people spend the most time with."***
>
> Jim Rohn

Be very cautious about who you spend your time with because if the words spoken to you and around you are destructive, then that's something you need to protect yourself against.

You want people that give you honest and challenging feedback. Undoubtedly you do. Yes, you want cheerleaders, but we need people who challenge us too, because from the challenge comes change.

When we're looking at confidence, you certainly don't want it to spill into arrogance or an inflated ego. You need people who will check you and be real with you.

But when people are undermining you, cutting you down, and telling you explicitly that you mean "f*** all", you've got to be cautious about who you're spending your time with when you're in the process of building your confidence.

---

*As a side note, I don't believe that confidence is something that you attain, then you tick a box, and it's done. Ticked and off we go on to the next thing. No, it's not like that. I believe that confidence ebbs and flows at different stages in life. It's something that I personally have gone through my ups and downs, ins and outs, twists and turns with. But I now know what, and who, to turn to in order to help build my confidence. And sometimes that is actually a lot of time on my own processing, reflecting, and feeding my mind with nourishing and good information.

Find Your Top 5 Points And Activate Them

It's vital in life to know the value that you bring. But for many people, they don't recognise their strengths and don't fully appreciate what they can do with these strong points. And for others, they simply can't bring themselves to say things like, "I'm a great listener," "I'm really funny," or "I'm naturally competitive meaning I thrive working in a sales environment."

> *"Magic is believing in yourself. If you can make that happen, you can make anything happen."*
>
> Johann Wolfgang Von Goethe

So, when I've worked with people in the past, I'll start by asking them to think of someone who admires them. Someone aged over 16 —and it can't be an animal! Your grandmother, your best friend, your co-worker…we've all got someone around us who looks up to us.

Then we begin an important practice. A practice you've probably never done before, but could be a game-changer for you…

Ask the person who admires you to share with you the five positive points they admire in you.

It could be that you're: kind, funny, empathetic, a great communicator etc. Once you have those five key qualities written down, what are you going to do with them? So now that you're empathic, could it be that there's someone around you who needs a little bit more kindness? Could it be that you could volunteer with a local community group?

In the brilliant book, "Man's Search For Meaning," author and Austrian psychiatrist Viktor Frankl, wrote about his experiences in three concentration camps in the Holocaust.

Frankl explains that after the Holocaust, he worked as a psychiatrist with people experiencing depression to whom he encouraged to volunteer in the local communities and libraries. He writes:

"As soon as people could fill their abundant free time with some sort of unpaid but meaningful activity, their depression disappeared."

Please note the word meaningful —an activity that has a point.

One of the United Kingdom's greatest leaders, Winston, Churchill said, "We make a living by what we get, but we make a life by what we give".

So, let's look at creating your life. To be clear, I am not suggesting you go and give everything, we looked at caregivers and often in love we can give too much away of ourselves. But like me, working in the office, I knew I wasn't creating anything meaningful, and I didn't have much to give, I felt suppressed, day after day, month after month, year after year. Over time, that feeling in me *knew* something needed to change. So, when you consistently have a feeling that something needs to change, trust it, and make the change.

I know from personal experience, that when I'm giving, I'm fully living. Giving, serving, helping, and sharing makes me feel alive. Which is why I wanted to share this book with you – to help you with what makes you come alive. To help you find the very point of your life.

So, back to those five great points about you…

Once you are clear on what those points are, it's time to enhance them. Share them with someone, give them to someone, do something with them. If you are in a true place of low confidence, start with yourself. Build those points within.

If one of the points that person that admires you said is, "you're funny", then make yourself laugh. Feed that about yourself. Go and watch something hilarious. Put on a comedy show, call a friend who you can have a belly laugh with…give yourself some of what makes you thrive, and then begin to share it with others.

If they say "you're a quick problem solver" – who needs support in fixing a problem? Or dial that into yourself, what do you know you have not fixed in your life that you've been avoiding? Yes, we all have something.

Having looked at building what's within you, next I want to help you with strategies to *improve* your confidence.

It is important to remember that confidence cannot be built overnight. This is something you work on daily. As I do.

Just as you 'build your muscle' in a gym to get better glutes, abs, biceps, you must 'build your muscle' in your confidence.

Some top tips I find that help:

- Surround yourself with people, places, and products that raise your level of self-worth and remove anything that does the opposite.
- What builds confidence is focusing on what you *can do now*. What are you already good at and what action can you take to improve in other areas?
- You must be realistic about your strengths.
- Show compassion towards your limitations.
- Once you've identified your positive points, enhance and activate these points about you.
- Think independently.
- Be active.
- Take courageous risks.
- Make eye contact with people when you interact, put your phone down and fully engage.
- Live in the present.
- Improve self-talk (be kind in your mind).

- Notice your physicality (how you carry your body).
- Check your body language – it accounts for 55% of what is communicated. How you stand is vital (more on this in Chapter 4).
- Your tone of voice plays an important role in what you communicate (38%).
- Your words account for just 7% of what is communicated.
- Therefore, stand up, step up and be bold in how you present yourself.

CHALLENGING YOUR INNER CRITIC

Your internal critic can be your biggest enemy if you let it. It can make you feel that you aren't good enough but when you notice a critical pattern of thought emerging, you have to recognise it and challenge those thoughts. We have negative judgements about ourselves, but we must conquer ourselves to stop and recognise that these judgements are not helpful to us. When you learn to harness your internal monologue to be one of internal support, to be kind to your mind, then confidence, worthiness and happiness will follow naturally.

Let's start there: the journey to confidence, worthiness and happiness. Take action.

Emmeline Pankhurst, a suffragette (who's great-granddaughter Helen I spoke alongside at a Commonwealth event), said "deeds, not words."

We are well acquainted with the phrase 'actions speak louder than words.' But if you want anything to move your confidence, your life, your relationships, your health, you have to act.

Sternum up, head held high – step up and into your great life. Let's go.

Deeds, not words.

Chapter 3

FOCUS & DISCIPLINE

☆

The mood was low. There was a lot of tension between the crew. And I just had a feeling that something was going to go wrong on the boat.

I was exhausted. The three cold sores on my face told a story about how run-down I actually was. Some of the crew members had been arguing because we were all so exhausted and short-tempered.

We'd all been working for a yacht company on the launch of a new boat for the summer season around Europe. The company had a strict deadline for launch – but had left the organisation of everything extremely late.

I was brought on board to help in April and was thrust into the thick of things. The workload and therein hours stacked up day after day. Soon I was doing far more overtime than I would work in eight-hour days to get through what was needed to the launch – on a daily basis.

This was whilst we were travelling throughout Europe. Lots of traveling. Lots of late nights. But it wasn't just me that was working all hours. The crew were, drivers were, salespeople were, each of us was exacerbated to get the boat launched.

It wasn't right. It wasn't sustainable. And it was going to lead to trouble. We just didn't realise how serious it would be.

It was the day of a sea trial (the boating equivalent of a test drive in a car). The waters were particularly choppy. John took charge of the boat that morning, looking wiped out. He was on automatic pilot and probably hadn't had a good eight hours of sleep at night for at least two months.

Then disaster struck. A large wave hit, crashed against the side of the boat, and two people on board were sent flying. Smashing against the interior of the boat, both people were injured and hospitalised. One of them sustained a serious back injury and took six months in hospital before she recovered.

What went wrong? How did that trip end with such serious consequences?

John was more than capable of driving a boat safely and he'd been an important member of our boat launch team. If only he had been strong mentally and physically, if he'd been alert, and if only we as employees had focus on our wellbeing from the company leaders, our health and safety, as workers but also as people…I know that he would have been more astute in navigating choppy waters.

As a result, two people ended up in hospital because of the focus not being on employee wellbeing, at all. Thank goodness there wasn't a death that day, it could have been a very different outcome. The hospitalisation of people demonstrated that when focus is not sharp as it could (or should) be, then major accidents, health and safety incidents and potentially tragic situations can happen.

Lack of Focus and Discipline Will Take You Down A Wrong Path

When we don't have focus and discipline in our life, it's easy to get distracted by the wrong things at work or in daily life. For example, an online sale (we've all been there – thanks to targeted ads), making comparisons on social media, message notifications on our phone, by the unimportant. We've all been pulled away from work we really should be doing by online adverts or holidays. One minute we're just perusing a clothes store on the web, then 45 minutes later we're checking out and spending money that we don't really need to.

Lack of focus and numerous interruptions affect our effectiveness and impact at work and in daily life. An undisciplined mind means that simple tasks can take a long time to finish. When we're not focused, we're not as attentive to personal and professional relationships. This loss of attentiveness to people close you to, can create a lack of understanding of people close to you. And when we lose understanding in people, this leads to misunderstandings.

A lack of focus impacts your memory. We become forgetful, procrastinate or make errors which undermine our professional and personal credibility.

> **"Some people want it to happen, some wish it would happen, others make it happen."**
>
> Michael Jordan

It's so easy to get distracted when we don't have proper focus and proper discipline. When I set up my business, I knew the mission of what I wanted to do. To powerfully raise peoples' experience of work and daily life. That's my guiding light and reason for doing what I do. It keeps me focused.

This photo captures the feeling of being focused on your point (incidentally, this is my favourite place, the top of the Malvern Hills, Worcestershire).

So, what does achieving the correct level of focus and discipline require?

- Know the point of what you're doing.
- Create a guiding mission statement for where you need better focus.
- Set yourself attainable goals and milestones.
- Have the right information and people around you.
- Let people close to you know exactly what your focus is.

Discipline goes hand in hand with consistency too. With parents and families, it's important for them to be consistent with their children's behaviour. When you're teaching a child table manners, for example, you need to be consistent in how you're approaching that. Discipline and focus are important – otherwise, you're going to create unruly children. The same with your mind. It can either be unruly or lucid.

Similarly, if you've started a new workout programme at the gym, it's imperative that you stay disciplined in showing up and doing the work…even if you're out of shape and the workouts are more difficult than you expected.

And when your mind gets busy creating excuses about staying in bed longer because you need more sleep or saying things to yourself like "this doesn't seem to be working, there's not much difference in the mirror", then it's important to stay focused on the mission and remember that consistent effort brings results (and results don't happen overnight).

I x F = PR (Information x Focus Equals Your Personal Reality)

The valuable equation above, is igniting teaching by Tony Robbins, the world-renowned motivational speaker and pioneer of human potential.

The information that you look at and have around you, multiplied by your focus equals your personal reality. Ultimately, what you're focusing on in your life becomes your personal reality.

"People who fail, focus on what they have to go through; people who succeed focus on what it will feel like at the end."

Tony Robbins

To build a stronger PR for yourself, let's look at your life together:

1. *Are you happy with where you are in your career, your personal life, your everyday results? The best place to start, if you're serious about changing your personal reality, is reviewing what you're focusing on.*

Be honest with yourself here.

2. *How much Netflix or reality TV are you watching on a weekly, or even daily, basis?*

3. *Do you read poor-quality newspapers, salacious gossip, or spend too much time each day scrolling through your phone?*

If you know you aren't feeding your mind with quality information, over time, your personal reality is going to be a poor quality one. You can easily fill your day with a lot of noise, bustle, and nonsense. A simple equation for you to remember:

Nonsense in = nonsense out

What you feed your mind will become what you experience. *So*, if you consistently focus on good quality information, like educational podcasts, or esteemed books which will help you develop better ideas and behaviours, then your personal reality will undoubtedly be lifted in a positive direction.

Your brain is like a garden. It moves, it flows, it grows. You must look after your mind. Like a garden, it can grow wild with weeds, or it can be beautiful and blossoming. I know which I'd rather.

Focusing on good quality information is like tending to the garden, taking out the weeds, watering the colourful plants, and keeping everything neat and tidy. It becomes a great place to be and begins to blossom.

> **"There is nothing so disobedient as an undisciplined mind, and there is nothing so obedient as a disciplined mind."**
>
> Buddha

When your focus and mindset turn negative it takes a lot of discipline to transform your way of thinking – but it is possible. Let's look at how together.

To Avoid a Downward Spiral

Negative self-talk and focusing on that can lead to a negative downward spiral. You then find it challenging to maintain a positive outlook in your mind.

- Developing focus and a strong mindset takes consistent work. Like training muscles in the gym or learning a new language.
- Let's look at how to intervene when you feel that downward spiral setting in.

"You are what you do, not what you say you'll do."

Carl Gustav Jung

Focus on YOUR Positive Points

The more you are consciously aware of your positive points, and activating these in your work and daily life, the more you will use these points about you to contribute to your success.

Successful Self-Talk

If you have a challenging situation at work or in daily life and you let negative self-talk take over, this can lead to a downward spiral in mindset and prevent progress. Let's ensure that doesn't happen.

- Recognise that your negative self-talk is an issue.
- Shift your focus from where you are right now, to what you could be doing to achieve your goals.
- Be pragmatic, gain appropriate knowledge and take action.
- When you are taking action towards your goals (doing something), you feel better.
- When you feel good. You achieve more.

> **"How wonderful it is that nobody need wait a single moment before starting to improve the world."**
>
> Anne Frank

POWER QUESTIONS FOR YOUR BETTER FOCUS

1. Where specifically do you need more focus in your work or life?

2. How will we know you've reached the target of that focus?

3. How do you discipline yourself?

4. Where can you say 'no' more? When we say yes, it often means saying no to something to discipline your own life.

5. How does multitasking affect your focus?

6. Where can you discipline one thing at a time?

7. Where can you give a little focus to finish what you started? (to avoid overwhelm).

8. In which environment do you feel most productive?

9. What makes you forget to eat?

10. How will you tell if you have fallen off track? How will you get back on track?

11. Who are the 10 most fascinating people you know? Do you regularly spend time with fascinating people from different fields to your own?

Chapter 4

ROUTINE

"You are what you repeatedly do."

The words of Greek philosopher Aristotle. So simple, yet powerful.

With Aristotle's message in mind, your excellence a direct result of your habits. Equally, however, our failure and downfall are also consequences of our habits.

This is why routine is an important pillar in the work I do with people – and why I've dedicated this entire chapter to it. I love to strengthen people towards their excellence and success. Therefore, I look closely with people at: what are they repeatedly doing?

What is their daily routine?

I've studied the work of psychologist, Dr Steve Orma[1], who looks at the importance of having a routine in terms

---

[1] https://www.drorma.com/how-to-handle-early-morning-awakenings-updated/

of sleep patterns, weight management, and managing stress. These are vital factors in our lives.

Now, I want to be clear that when I create a routine with people, I don't create a rigid timetable. It's not like at school…where it's maths at 9am, then geography at 10am, then physical exercise at 11am, then lunch et cetera.

Your routine that we create here isn't going to be getting up at 6am, having a green juice, then the gym, then attending to emails at 8am, and phone calls at 9am. Routine can't be regimented – because life doesn't work like that.

We need flexibility in terms of how we approach life…because your dog could be ill. The children could have been up through the night. Your boss could need something urgently. We've got to be able to flex around life's changes, and not be too rigid in our routine. Otherwise, it adds pressure and stress, which is precisely what we're trying to break away from.

> **"When scientists analyse people who appear to have tremendous self-control, it turns out those individuals aren't all that different from those who are struggling. Instead, 'disciplined' people are better at structuring their lives in a way that does not require heroic willpower and self-control."**
>
> James Clear, Atomic Habits

Energy Givers & Takers

When I work on routine with people, I look closely at their energising habits and help structure their life better in accordance with what personally energises them. I'll conduct what Rich Litvin[2] – a world-leading coach's coach – describes as an 'energy audit'. It's very, very simple. We start with a piece of paper, and we draw a line down the middle. The left-hand side will become a list of what fills your energy. The right side we list what drains your energy.

Sometimes it's nature, or writing comedy, or spending time with family, enjoying the learnings of certain podcasts…or even time alone. Everybody has different energising habits. I find that an energy audit is an exercise that most people have never even considered doing before.

So, let's look closely at structuring a routine for your life, for you to be a more vibrant and full-hearted version of yourself. It's when we order our life like this that we are more capable of facing challenges, we have more of a spring in our step and can face life's darker times with more vitality and head-on. In concurrence with James Clear, when we do more of what brings out the very best in us, we don't need to dig so deep for willpower, we are living naturally at our best. I am very often asked "Where do you get your energy from?" The response is clear, I'm simply very aware of maintaining great energy and here's the important part, I *do*, what fills me with vibrant energy and limit what doesn't.

---

[2] https://richlitvin.com/wp-content/uploads/2018/08/Energy-Audit-Tool-bw.pdf

Next, let's look at the right-hand side column of what takes away energy. Now let's be real – we can't always eliminate everything that takes our energy. Often unexciting tasks do need our attention. Socks need pairing…and I don't know anyone that finds exhilaration from pairing socks. Sometimes, we've got to do mundane yet vital tasks …but there will always be an opportunity to discern what doesn't serve you by looking at what takes your energy. This exercise helps understand yourself better for creating a routine for your life that energises and fulfils you.

More on energy later.

For now, let's get back to habits and what we repeatedly do.

While positive habits in your daily routine will obviously build better, more productive days. The reverse is also true. If you're repeatedly opening the fridge door, taking a bite of this, taking a bite of that, and then sitting on the sofa to binge-watch something, then that's going to show up in your life.

What you do in private shows up in public. It's going to show if you're constantly snacking and not moving so much. Whereas if you're active, you're going to feel better and have more vibrancy.

Similarly, if you want to learn a language, like Mandarin for example, you have to repeatedly practice, listen to, and speak new words. You need to create a new habit. You're not just going to do it once and wake up the next morning and then be fluent in Mandarin. What we repeatedly do creates habits, skills, and furthers our personal development.

> ***"You are what you repeatedly do. Excellence therefore is a habit"***
>
> Aristotle

Key Areas Of Focus In Your Routine

Physicality is an important area of focus in your routine. Now this doesn't simply mean going to the gym and working out to strengthen your body and mind. But what are you doing with your body language? A lot of people come to me with confidence issues. They're dealing with imposter syndrome or feeling a bit stuck or don't fully understand the value they bring to the world.

I love helping people develop through a whole host of confidence issues, as I've been there with low confidence, from not being valued in relationships to working in environments that I feel I don't belong, to social dynamics that can make you feel you don't matter. This is why I'm resolutely passionate about each pillar we're journeying through together in this book, I want to help you find your full life, you at your most alive and the point of your precious and valuable life.

We all know that when we're in a place of low confidence, feeling stuck, and lacking direction, we tend to slump. With that kind of posture, we are not at our most alive. Your physicality plays such an essential part in life. Dr. Albert Mehrabian's detailed research[3] on physicality generated the 7-38-55 rule. The 7-38-55 rule shows that just 7% of all communication is via your verbal communication (the words you choose), whereas the nonverbal aspects (tone of your voice and your body language) of your daily communication, account for 38% and 55% respectively of your communication's impact.

Consider then that 55% of what you communicate is through your body language. Your stance and body movement therefore are more impactful than the words you chose and how you say those words.

Firstly, let's not forget that how you communicate, is to yourself. Look at the story you're telling *yourself*. If you're spending a lot of your time slumped over, with low energy, lacking vibrancy, and low physicality, then you're communicating to yourself that low and lacklustre is acceptable – and lacklustre becomes the status quo for you.

You can change this. You can show up with greater vibrancy in the world. Raise your heart in your chest. Do that now.

---

[3] https://www.businessballs.com/communication-skills/mehrabians-communication-theory-verbal-non-verbal-body-language/

"Courage, the original definition of courage, when it first came into the English language — it's from the Latin word cor, meaning heart — and the original definition was to tell the story of who you are with your whole heart."

Brené Brown[4]

So, to have courage, we need to bring our heart forward. Lift your heart up in your chest, your collarbones naturally then rise, your shoulders go back and you show courage. That simple posture shift changes your body language totally.

Another key area of focus is your evening habits. People I work with often tell me that they want to start getting up early to go to the gym in the morning, to meditate, journal or whatever morning practice is trendy at that moment. My response is always the same: "How can we sort your morning if your evening routine isn't properly in practice?"

Some people spend their evenings gaming. Others do online shopping. Some people spend them watching porn until the small hours.

---

4 https://www.ted.com/talks/brene_brown_the_power_of_vulnerability?language=en

Sakari Lemola, whilst assistant professor of psychology at the University of Warwick, discovered through his research when looking at technology use that people using smartphones fall asleep later at night. "This is probably because they're engaging with social media, communicating with friends and watching YouTube," Lemola said.

Fascinatingly, his research established that, "electronic media use around bedtime was related to decreased sleep duration and increased symptoms of insomnia. Short sleep and poor sleep quality were in turn related to depressive symptoms[5]."

There are several possible connections, Lemola found that modern flat screens emit a larger amount of blue light, which suppresses melatonin. This is a hormone created by your pineal gland at night or in the dark that regulates your circadian rhythm, (your internal body clock) and therein your energy. So, the more melatonin you suppress by screen time at night, the more depleted your energy becomes.

With teenagers and adults alike being kept up late at night – with faces glued to our screens, are you giving yourself the best chance of a strong morning routine? Remember that workout you wanted to do? Or updates to a work project? Or spending better quality time with the children over breakfast? Too much screen time diminishes a healthy and vibrant routine for you. This is why I always

---

[5] https://www.scientificamerican.com/article/are-smartphones-really-destroying-the-lives-of-teenagers/

structure what a resilient evening routine looks like before trying to design a healthy, powerful morning routine.

A few years ago, I had a client who came to me at a time when he was stuck career wise, weight wise, marriage wise… key areas of his life were causing him worry, he lacked direction and certainly motivation with how to move forward. Dissatisfied with his job. No vibrancy in his relationship and he desperately wanted my support in how to improve these juxtaposed areas of his life.

He wanted to start running in the morning to improve his health, lose some weight, and feel better about himself. He also wanted to be able to spend more time with his wife and work on the relationship.

When we looked at his evening routine and it wasn't long before we discovered a problem. After much discussion about his behaviours and habits, we exposed that his mobile phone use was engulfing his time and energy in the evening. He was using it far more than he actually realised, and it was impacting his life in various (negative) ways.

We introduced a little 'phone box' for his house, which is simply a cheap and cheerful basket. He and his partner were to put their phones in this phone box at a certain time every evening – and I would hold him accountable.

Day after day, week after week of doing this, the man reclaimed many hours which he'd been giving away each day. He and his wife had more meaningful time together, building their connection back together again. And he wasn't getting so much blue light from his mobile phone screen – which as you now know, suppresses the production of melatonin and supports your energy rhythms around the clock. This meant he was achieving a more restful sleep at night and was then able to wake up earlier and exercise in the morning, developing a positive morning routine.

Another client I supported, a highly intellectual man who was a leader in a high-performance and high-pressure business, was becoming frustrated because he simply wasn't finding enough time for reading books on leadership. He was keen to develop his leadership style but was simply not finding the time to study how to.

The approach we took in his sessions together, was to break his goal down into manageable daily habits for him. I worked with him to begin reading just 10 pages of his book every evening before bed. Not a chapter. Not 50 pages. Just 10 pages and no more. It was a simple commitment and, most importantly, it gave him a routine to help augment his skills so that he was better equipped to lead his team with efficiency, stability, compassion and power.

For me personally, a vital part of my daily routine is a morning workout. I know that I have an elevated day when I work out in the morning, it focuses my mindset, gives me vibrancy and starts the day with success. That's a foundational part of my routine and it's what gets me out of bed each day. I often give myself weekends off, but on a weekday this routine encourages me to get out of bed. I know that I'll be a better person at four o'clock in the afternoon if I have an energy slump and a challenging email appears to reply to, or a difficult conversation to be having, if I've worked out in the morning.

This part of my routine means I'm far more equipped psychologically and emotionally to tackle things head on. And for me, that's the key reason that I do it. A workout promotes my mental fitness, my psychological strength. Of course, the physical part is important, but what's even more important is how my brain ignites and is fired up by doing a workout in the morning.

What also gives me energy is learning and making progress. Whether it's in sports, through my work with clients or from a new book that I've read, learning and making progress brings me energy. Equally, watching my clients thrive and seeing that something we've worked on together has accelerated and impacted their life for the greater good, genuinely gives me real-jumping-around-cartwheels-kind-of-energy.

Protecting Your Energy

As we bring this chapter on routine into land and you implementing positive habits, I want to touch upon some 'energy takers' which I'm very aware of. I feel it's important for all of us to protect our energy to show up as your most vibrant and enriched self for your work and daily life.

Personally, what takes energy here is being around too many negative people, too much of the time. Of course, there are countless negative people, and we have to handle them, and often help them – but you have the power to limit that type of contact. Being surrounded, consistently by negativity is not good for your soul and spirit.

Secondly, bad food choices really lower my energy levels. At the same time, I love a birthday celebration and all the foods that go with it, that's called living. But I know that if I've eaten too much sugar and/or processed foods, I just feel in a low mood and unexciting. It doesn't help my psyche at all.

With this journey through improving your routine, it's vital that you get clear on what gives you energy and what takes it away. What makes you thrive and what makes you feel like an inspired version of yourself? This precision in your life will give you stronger direction as you move forward.

Ultimately, grasping your robust routine equates to greater freedom and improved happiness for you.

You are what you repeatedly *do* after all.

POWER QUESTIONS FOR YOUR BETTER ROUTINE

1. Describe a time when you felt consistency in your life?

2. What habits energise you?

3. What does a good evening routine look like to you?

4. Do you do anything in your evening to create your morning routine?

5. When do you check your phone in the morning?

6. What 1-3 habits drain you of the most energy?

7. What are your keystone habits? These are teeny habits that have a huge impact on your life (e.g. hiring a personal trainer, no junk food in the house, no phone in the bedroom, tracking your expenditures, flossing before you brush your teeth).

8. What are you trying to get perfect before taking action in your daily routine?

Chapter 5

FULFILMENT

☆

It was a Saturday night in December, and I received a phone call which would change the entire course of my life. I never actually answered that call. I was busy, not aware that Tom had been trying to reach me.

We were teenagers then and Tom was a close and dear friend. Nothing romantic, just a strong, trusting, caring and supportive friendship. We went to different schools, and yet we'd check in with each other regularly and talk about all life's colours like our aspirations, friendships, our family dynamics, our insecurities, what was holding us back, the challenges we experienced and the pressures of the future. We'd send each other cards of encouragement for events in our lives, we were good and kind friends together.

I ardently yearn to have answered his call that night. The next morning, my mother sat with me at the kitchen table and said, "Last night, Tom took his life." And my number had been the last dialled on his phone.

So, then I became involved with police and the inquest into his death.

Knowing that I wasn't there when he really needed me to be, has impacted my life in the most profound way. I have a deep hunger to be there for people because it's too late for Tom. In fact, I called my company Lift This Life because I didn't lift *his* life when he truly needed it.

So now, everything I work towards is Tom's legacy to me. The core of that work is to substantially uplift the people that I encounter in my work and daily life. So, fulfilment for me has such deep resonance. My work is my deep fulfilment and I thus know how important it is for others to find. Call it "fulfilment" or the point of your life… THIS is why I created this fifth paramount pillar in my work.

In fact, now, I define success as knowing a life has breathed easier because of my existence. Because it is too late now for Tom to breathe again.

People that are on the edge of suicide, struggling with depression or anxiety, are not feeling fulfilment, or indeed meaning or "the point" in their lives.

So, fulfilment for me has such deep resonance.

I love to help people discover what genuinely fulfils them – and crucially experience more of that, powerfully in their life. Several years ago, I took part in a human potential seminar, and I learned a pivotal philosophy from Tony Robbins which is: "Success without fulfilment is the ultimate failure."

Read that twice and let it land.

In society, we are encouraged to find our success. Personally, I've been driven to be surrounded by the very best in my career, whether that's working on Top Gear, with Rolls-Royce Motor Cars, or during my time working on The Olympic Games. I've always been motivated to experience the very pinnacle of industry.

When I learnt that success without fulfilment is the ultimate failure, it resonated profoundly as I've witnessed deep unfulfillment in all walks of life and this made me reconsider how I navigate my own life.

Yet, over the years, with non-governmental organisations for the marginalised, including working in the slums of India with communities where people have nothing, literally nothing, (so much so that they even steal electricity) — you should see how!) They don't chase success. They chase community. They chase people and find enrichment, meaning and their point through that.

With children in Mumbai, India.

I've observed children in India playing with a tiny toy car that you pull back a few times, and it accelerates when you let it go. This one simple toy has entertained 15 children at a time. There they are fulfilled by togetherness, and community, by being with each other and playing, in extreme poverty.

Fulfilment for everyone looks very different. When I heard that success without fulfilment is the ultimate failure, it felt a game-changing philosophy. You see, I've worked with people who society says are successful, famous, wealthy, large followings on social media and yet I've also witnessed some deeply unfulfilled behaviours in these environments.

Having spent some of my career in the media and in the company of celebrities to sporting personalities, and indeed when employed with Rolls-Royce Motor Cars, I'd encountered many 'very successful' people (success in terms of wealth).

And yet, I've seen drugs, alcoholism, rudeness, infidelity, and disrespect – these aren't behaviours synonymous with people who are happy or fulfilled.

Thus, I've witnessed many unfulfilled behaviours from what many people view as highly successful people.

Hence, these experiences emphasised the importance of focusing on fulfilment for the people I work with and for you too reading this book.

Isabella Blow and Caroline Flack, both British icons of the media, created excitement, joy and delight for others yet both ladies struggled with depression. We saw their outward success, the vibrancy that these ladies crafted in their own light for everybody else…but neither Isabella nor Caroline had crafted fulfilment, created a brightness or a guiding light within themself. And both people, tragically in different circumstances ended their own life.

Developing people in their fulfilment – the substance and true richness of their life – drives of my work. Helping people authentically discover what truly enriches and invigorates their work and daily life is my friend Tom's powerful legacy to me.

Finding Fulfilment In Your Life: The Starting Point

'How do I find fulfilment in my own life?'

'Where do I even begin?'

You may be asking yourself these questions at this juncture.

When I work with people, I've developed a series of specific discovery questions around fulfilment in life. I delve into this area with people to begin a process of self-realisation and draw out valuable and profound meaning from within. To clarify this, there is one pivotal question which absolutely spearheads the search for fulfilment…

What do you do on a daily basis that's meaningful for you?

Emphasis on the word 'you' at the end. Because if you're not doing something meaningful for you each day, then you are not fully living your life.

A couple of years ago I was working with a business leader, let's call her Laura (not her real name, as client confidentiality is paramount) who was feeling entirely pressurised in her work. If she didn't get things right, death could occur, there would be legal implications, people could go to prison, the company would go out of business. We're talking about serious implications in her very serious role.

I worked with Laura because she was struggling with strength in her leadership. She was experiencing family issues at home, and equally, she was struggling with her work performance. The sensitive and shattering health concerns in her family at home were impacting her performance at work. As a result, her leadership needed focus because she was (and still is) leading within a high-profile organisation.

With the understanding of everything that she was experiencing within her family life at home and the enormous stress in her workplace, I knew that developing her in what enriched her from the inside would strengthen her personally and be hugely beneficial to her work and daily life.

In one of our sessions together, I asked Laura: "What do you do on a daily basis that's meaningful for you?"

She paused.

She breathed deeply.

And then she cried.

After wiping away the tears and composing herself again, Laura replied: "Nothing."

The question had caught her off guard. She'd never properly contemplated how little she'd been doing for herself in her life.

Her job and its pressures had taken priority. As had the issues at home, taking care of the family, driving them to medical appointments, managing their drug and dosage changes and then the repercussions on family life.

Laura doing something meaningful for herself each day hadn't been a thought. This was a bold realisation for her.

In response, I asked her: "Do you therefore feel that you are living YOUR life?"

Her tears were a warning sign that fulfilment in her own life was what we needed to pay attention to, so she could find her own strength in living fully. We needed to find her strength and meaning within she could shine brighter, from the inside out, both personally and professionally.

I knew that we really had to plug into was precisely what would bring her life fulfilment.

For Laura, it was important to find what connected her with herself again. I know of no better method than through yoga practice. After a great friend Maria, encouraged me to do yoga following three knee operations, I felt the benefits of regular practice so I have trained to teach yoga so I can share its magic. Yoga the word means 'to yoke' so is a union and reconnection of body, mind and spirit. This is through movement and breathe practice.

*With valued friend Maria in Madrid
who encouraged practicing yoga.*

Breathing is vital, well it is what gives us life. It's the first thing we do when we're born, and last thing before we die- and yet in between we don't give it that much focus! We take on average 25000 breaths a day[6], so giving daily time to this life-giving force works wonders for you.

Back to Laura, we started her practicing yoga just once a week – because that's all she could find time for in the beginning.

Now Laura is practicing yoga three times a week and has found it hugely beneficial for looking after herself, and reconnecting with her brain, body and breath. We are still connected today where she's leading and loving her family with re-ignited strength.

---

6 https://www.asthmaandlung.org.uk/how-your-lungs-work

Charles Schulz, famed for creating the Peanuts cartoons, said: "There's no heavier burden than an unfulfilled potential".

Knowing what's inside you, what you're capable of and what brings meaning your life and crucially doing that is transformative in finding your life's rich fulfilment.

Crucially though, to feel this abundantly, take active steps to pragmatically do what's meaningful for you. Carve out time to live the meaning to your life. This will keep the point of your life alive. And then it's something you can pass on to the next generations.

This book is called, What's The Point? and it's in this particular fulfilment pillar where you'll find the point of your life. This is it.

Tom would ask me frequently, "What's the point of life?" – and if you've ever searched for this, it is my earnest hope that this book helps you answer that for yourself.

To be clear, I can't tell people what the point of their life is, but I can certainly help people discover that and do more of it. And for our great leader, Laura, the point of her life is not yoga. It was about finding out who she is, what's within her psychologically and activating what brings her life true meaning. For her, meaning and fulfilment is about using the psychological strength within her (to which, our work together connected her) and crucially for her, having a happy and healthy family.

Yes, she's a phenomenal leader. Undeniably, she's brilliantly successful in her industry. But when her life really comes down to the crunch, the point of her life is her family being happy and healthy.

Everyone you'll encounter has a different point to their life. For example, I work with a lawyer and for her, and her husband, it's having a Ferrari and a second home in the south of France. Each person is distinct in what drives them in life, and what point is of their life. It is not my place to judge where people find their succour, it is my place and life's work to help people find what brings their life meaning and, crucially, help get them there. This I take very seriously.

What Makes You Come Alive?

A life-giving philosophy I like to live by is from Martin Luther King Jr.'s mentor Howard Thurman, who was a civil rights activist. He powerfully said:

> *"Don't ask yourself what the world needs. Ask yourself what makes you come alive. Because what the world needs is people who have come alive."*

What is it that makes you come alive? What are you passionate about? It might be pioneering an innovation, advancing technology for good, a social cause, or work to enhance your local community. It could even be a charitable move caused by personal experience, for example, supporting a heart charity because a family member had a heart attack.

For me, suicide prevention is a driver of my life and I find this cause fulfilling to pursue. Indeed, the people I encounter, I like to help them experience the richness and full colour of life.

To add to this, I understand how powerfully laughing enriches the soul. Proper belly laughs, remember those? Laughter is scientifically proven through serotonin activation to reduce depressive symptoms[7] I love to laugh so I frequently watch comedy and encourage people around me to also.

Subsequently, to deepen your fulfilment and discovery of the point of your life, poignant questions for you to consider:

What causes make you passionate?

What do you become more animated talking about?

Write your personal responses down and focus on them in your life…because right there you'll discover and live more of what makes you come alive.

When asking yourself, "What's The Point?" it's in the answer to those questions that you'll find the point of your life. Then you can share the point of your life.

---

[7] https://synapse.koreamed.org/articles/1003058

Winston Churchill, one of the United Kingdom's greatest leaders said: "We make a living by what we get, but we make a life by what we give."

Where you find your life's point, consider how you truly live it and then pass it on to others around you.

Poet Mary Oliver said, "Tell me, what are you going to do with your one wild and precious life?"

Indeed, what are you going to do with your one life? Let's agree that you do what it is that makes you come alive, so you can live your authentic and most fulfilled life.

This is precisely what I want for you.

POWER QUESTIONS TO FIND YOUR FULFILMENT

1. What do you do on a daily basis that is meaningful to you?

2. What did your 8-year-old self love doing?

3. What issues do you hold close to your heart?

4. What news stories really compel you?

5. What do you value?

6. What is on your bucket list?

7. What 3 top things do you enjoy doing?

8. If you were fully living the point of your life, what would you be doing right now?

Chapter 6

SUCCESS & SUSTAINABILITY

By this sixth pillar on our journey together, you're already well on your way to discovering the point of your life and your best opportunity for success. You've been equipped with five powerful pillars in each of the previous chapters that will help you overcome blocks to living a richer, more authentic life.

But when you achieve the success you've been craving, how will you maintain it? How will you sustain the positive habits and the right attitude to keep moving forward?

Success and sustainability are the key themes in the final pillar of this book because, while I'll always be cheering you onto be ALL you can be, I also aim to equip you with what you need for your life.

You see, I consider what I do as a professional service, like when you need a lawyer. You only need that legal expert to journey alongside you for a certain period of your life, whatever it is you're going through. Similarly, with my work, you've been given solid strength and support – and then you're equipped with ways to rely on to live a fulfilled, passionate and dazzling life.

That's what I want to do: to give people the tools, frameworks, and techniques so that they become stronger. It's to help people get clear on their value in the world – and then set sail with the artillery and better thinking that I've shared.

My objective is not to work with people for the long term. It's to equip them with what they need for a stronger, more fulfilled, and uplifted life.

As we build towards your success, when we started chapter one with clarity, the focus was on defining the vision for your life.

What does success look like?

Are we there?

Are we near where we said we wanted to be?

We might not be – and this isn't a performance review, or performance management in the workplace. But we've put frameworks in place to get you there, more effectively.

Then with sustainability…it's in terms of momentum. How do we keep the impact and motion of what we've worked on together moving forward? Some clients, for their sustainability, do stay with me for years for their strength and support. That's where they feel that they want to continue working together on a fortnightly or monthly basis. And I'm not here to say no to people, I'm here to help people say yes to more from work and daily life. Some people do want the sustainability, the accountability, and the energy that I create with them.

So, when we embark upon this final pillar, it's not a closing of the door and off you go. It's making sure we have got the correct tools in place for progress and momentum to life at the next level.

I've been working with a fabulous tech leader for years now. What we do together is very much part of her personal and business growth. As the great and late Jim Rohn said, "You are the product of the five people you spend the most time with" – and this wisdom is key to building success and sustainability with my client.

Every six months with her, we do an analysis, and ask: who are your five people? Because life changes for everybody and every six months, we sensor check that she is surrounded by the most energising, inspiring and strong people she can be.

Who are your five people? These can include colleagues, friends, authors, speakers, researchers, and sometimes it's a podcast host for this particular client who best strengthens her development at that time.

I worked with another sensational leader who was not getting promoted because of pre-existing (and very limiting) beliefs about herself. She'd been brought up in a very challenging environment, with social services having been involved in her upbringing, and her family were involved in crime at a high level. As a result, she was taken away from her family and into care at aged 10.

She found a job within an exciting organisation and her boss cited her as a future leader due to:

1. The way that she cared about people.
2. The approach she took in passionately developing people within her team.

However, her boss couldn't promote her because her confidence in herself was not what he saw. She believed that – because of the conditions that she'd been brought up in, crime, poverty, etc. – she wasn't worth being promoted. She didn't believe that she was valuable enough because of the environment that she'd been brought up in.

She didn't know that she was good enough to be a leader within the workplace or within the world.

This meant her boss asked me to work with her on combating the limiting beliefs that she held about herself. Her pre-existing experiences. The life that she'd had. The past that she'd endured…that didn't have to be her future. We took the reins; I worked with her and took her through this six-pillar process that you've been following in this book.

> **"We are not creatures of circumstance; we are creators of circumstance."**
>
> Benjamin Disreali, *Prime Minister (twice) of The United Kingdom*

We had to position her mindset away from the circumstances she'd been brought up in, into what she could create for herself. And we did.

Fast forward a few years, she brought me in to work with her new team too. That's because she's developed from a local role to a global position, looking after people in the organisation, leading teams throughout countries around the world.

Throughout her progress, we really worked hard at combating her belief systems – and challenging how she feels about herself, crucially, and how she can create better for herself and discover the true point of her life – which is developing stronger people around her. Now, she's authentically setting the world on fire through her people with great success.

'I Can Do Better Than This!'

It's easy to fall back into negative behaviours and old habits, of course. But having gone through this framework, I think people are equipped with the tools, mindset, and techniques to BE better and DO better.

Personally, I stay in touch with many people that I work with, whether it's an email check-in, or a phone call for updates. I like to keep in communication as it means there's always that level of accountability with me.

In fact, I actually consider what I do with people as '*kicking ass, with compassion*'. And let's be real with each other, we all need a kick up the botty at times. I know I do.

Leadership Development at Bentley Motors

To let you know how I operate personally, there is one (of many) simple and practical way to stay accountable to the things that I've promised myself. One way that I give myself a kick, and consistently live my own message – is by putting meaningful reminders in my phone.

I have three reminders on my phone on a daily basis. I have one at 7am to keep my mindset strong and looking up.

1. When I've woken up, and have just worked out, the first reminder chimes at 7am, saying: "I can do better than this."

So, if the mind starts wandering in the wrong direction, if I think about eating some processed food for breakfast, or if I decide to be lazy and not get much done, that message will remind me that "I can do better than this."

2. At 12.30pm I have one of Brené Brown's quotes appearing, which is: "Today, I choose courage over comfort."

This one encourages that I ask myself, "What's the courageous move here?" Every day it is different. Rather than going with the comfortable move after lunchtime, when I've had some difficult emails or something frustrating has happened to throw my day out of kilter, this reminder (thanks to Brené) invites me to step up and step into more for the afternoon, rather than write the rest of the day off because something troublesome has happened in the morning – which I've done.

That would be the easy thing, to surrender, but courage comes through practice and this daily reminder at lunchtime invites a bolder and brighter way of living.

I have to be honest, of course there will occasionally be days when I choose comfort over courage. I'm not 100% perfect. But these little reminders can be powerful for instilling positive habits, keeping you on track, and building momentum.

3. Then in the evening, at 7.30pm, a little mantra goes off, "I expand in abundance, success and love every day – and inspire those around me to do the same."

This one reminder is what it's all for, to live a life that's uplifted and encouraging the people I encounter to do the same. That's the point of my life and what success is to me, to know that others have breathed better because of my existence – thanks to my friend Tom.

I'd like to invite you to consider your own success…in a really personal, profound way. By this, I mean take some time to think about what's really important in your life. What would be a real measurement of success in your life?

There are not set rules – because this is your personal success. Not your father's success. It's not what would make your mother proud, or what she wants for your life. It's not what your children want for you…or what your employer sees as success for you.

It's what YOU want for your life. This is where we find the point of our lives. And this, at our core, is when we are fully alive.

POWER QUESTIONS TO YOUR SUCCESS

1. What obstacles do you need to overcome to put your point into place?

2. Can you recall a time that you implemented a new behaviour into your life? How did you do it?

3. How close are you to your definition of success?

4. What works well for you to maintain momentum of energy?

5. What are you doing that someone else should be doing?

6. What are you avoiding doing?

7. What are some milestones you will have on the way to fully living the point of your life?

8. How will you feel once you have succeeded?

CONCLUSION

> *"The content of your character is your choice. Day by day, what you choose, what you think and what you do is who you become."*
>
> Heraclitus

I am deeply optimistic about people's ability to change their life from one of mediocrity to creating the extraordinary. Working in prisons to rehabilitate offenders for a second chance in life, I see and feel the exceptional potential for people to live fruitful, transformed, and more meaningful lives. Whether it's in a prison or in a boardroom, I love to help people find their strength and value to powerfully raise experience of work and daily life.

So, being fully alive in living the point of your life refines to what exactly?

Your choices.

You can choose to take the learnings of this book and activate them in your work and daily life. You can choose to use this book to improve your career, your relationships, your inner strength, your vitality and your value in the world.

And yet, I know making improved choices and great changes to your life, i.e. realising and living the point of your life is not an overnight process or the wave of a magical wand.

Stanford Professor of Psychology Carol Dweck describes a "growth mindset" or the concept that proficiency in work and daily life can be 'grown' through effort and learning – so as we bring this book into land, here is your opportunity to choose to grow.

Throughout your reading of "What's The Point" the six-pillar framework I've taken you through is designed sequentially and neatly to be a basis for you to powerfully develop the point of your life.

It's a framework which at best, will establish and help you realise the point of your life. At the very least, it is my earnest hope that this framework will have improved you in asking poignant questions to uplift your work and daily life.

Often, we lose our learnings when we realise our personal answers to questions are challenging to put into daily practice. Frequently, I'll say to people, "Where there is a challenge, there is a change."

So, in being the point of your life, you must commit to giving it your all.

There is one easy framework to living an unfulfilled and unexciting life with no real point to it, and that's to, *stay the same* and *do nothing*. The steps to living an enriched life are not easy or straightforward, as I said in my introduction to you. And yet, you're my kind of "Carpe Diem" person, aren't you? So, let's take the reins and kick on.

Let's look at how we maximise the point of your life. In simple terms, you must care about it enough and share it. Scientific research[8], shows that we a biologically hardwired to care for others. Compassion is a natural attribute; the world and experiences can harden us not to care. Science shows compassion is what we naturally do. In research around empathy and social behaviour, rodents are moved to help and care for a struggling rat, they'll move to support another. The studies even show rats will share their chocolate with another who is struggling.

I don't know about you, but I love chocolate and I don't often share it! In seriousness, science shows it's in biological DNA to care and share, so care about what you do and let it have a ripple effect.

You're the kind of person who KNOWS there is more for you from life. So what are you waiting for? Let's live the point of our life for ourselves and the betterment of others. Fully. Living it.

---

[8] https://www.drorma.com/how-to-handle-early-morning-awakenings-updated/

> ***"Honey, may you also choose to give up the prison and do the work to be free. To find in your suffering your life lessons. To choose which legacy the world inherits. To hand down the pain – or to pass on the gift."***
>
> Dr. Edith Eger, *Eminent psychologist and Holocaust survivor*

You *fully* living the point of your life. What's that going to feel like?

A block to freely living the point of your life and passing it on is simply not letting yourself *live* the point of your life. Choosing to stay stuck in a place of pain or fear. Hour by hour, day by day, you make your choices. Moving forward from now, my encouragement is you choosing to fully live the point of life that you desire. Make your life a gift, to yourself and others.

Living from your heart, which is where I believe you find your passion and the point of your life, is not the easy or soft way. This new way takes repeating habits, making better choices and many 'learning experiences' (aka mistakes) to robustly realise the point of your life.

Buddhist monk Thích Nhất Hạnh said, "The longest journey you will ever take is the 18 inches from your head to your heart."

Just let that sink in.

Another block in experiencing the true point of YOUR life is thinking that something or someone will come to save or help you. One event or person — a seminar, a new boss, this (or any) book, a philosopher, the right partner, an award, or a new home will cement the point of your life.

Whilst these factors may form some of the point of your life, at best, they add to the colour of your life. Believing in a fairy tale (and worse, trying to live one), that someone or an event will cement the point of our life, will lead us to frustration and emptiness.

> *"The meaning of life is to find your gift. The purpose of life is to give it away."*
>
> Pablo Picasso

The point of your life is seized by your commitment, consistency and choices.

The more we fill each day with commitment, consistency and choices positioned within the point of our life, the more completely alive we are.

Now moving forward, let's live the point of life, and passionately pass it on.

ABOUT THE AUTHOR

Dani Grieveson is a developer of people, business leader, writer and podcaster based in the West Midlands area of the United Kingdom.

Dani's career started on Top Gear. Blowing up sheds, caravans and testing automobiles to their absolute limit while working within a dynamic and globally celebrated team. Using her drive to create strength and success with people meant she worked with The Olympic Games, Coca-Cola and Rolls-Royce Motor Cars.

Not only has Dani worked for high profile businesses but she has devoted her time to humanitarian work helping victims of abuse and neglect restart their lives. Dani was invited to be a guest lecturer for the military delivering on leadership at the Defence Academy of the United Kingdom.

Passionately developing people, she lifts productivity, confidence and performance in an upbeat yet compassionate style.

Outside of lifting life, Dani enjoys stand-up comedy, family time and volunteering with a mental health trust.

You can see her website at:

www.danigrieveson.com

PRAISE OF DANI GRIEVESON'S WORK

"Her training methods build on our team's strengths and their confidence and result in people feeling positive and capable of facing any challenge, head on. She is reliable, honest, fun and fair – she is a little rocket that will bring out the very best in your people."

Justin Pegg, *Chief Operating Officer, DPDgroup UK*

"She gave me lots of useful tips and tricks for my day-to-day job. We kept in touch and Dani remembered all my big milestones at work or life in general and she's just capable of spreading all this amazing energy over to you. She's a great listener and her ideas and suggestions have enabled me to immediately make an impact and I am so grateful to have her."

Amelie Wieland, *Business Manager, Tesla*

"Our sessions with Dani are intelligently researched, based on my specific business needs and the personal strengths psychology of each person in my team. This has helped confidence, communication and engagement levels at work. Working with Dani throughout the year, we developed better trust and connection plus discovered new ways to engage at work which has lifted business productivity, profitability and performance."

Adam Hewitt, *Managing Director, Adam Hewitt Ltd*

"Dani honestly changed my life in 8 weeks. She worked with me to understand my personal strengths and how I could use and work with these to move my career and personal life forward. Dani has a wonderful and positive nature and has an extraordinary way of making you feel like you are her only client. She becomes almost like your own personal cheerleader. I found that I left her sessions with a clear plan and motivation to be better."

Laura Bailey, *People and Culture Leader*

"Dani's coaching gets better than expected results, fast. She is an excellent listener who quickly sees through any situation and with her razor-sharp observations and questions, guides through any tricky work issues, while looking at it from a holistic view. A session with her brings instant and great relief and a sense of balance all over again."

Strategy Director, *Global Technology Business*

"Daniella's approach and drive for others are invigorating to be around. She has uncovered and enriched my strengths, so I am increasingly effective in what I do."

CEO, Engineering

"Dani has had an incredible impact on my life. She has helped me understand my strengths, values and find my purpose. This has given me a new found energy to progress both personally and professionally. I contacted her feeling lost and lacking direction but every interaction we have leaves me energised. Dani is a fireball of positivity and there is no one else you'd be better within your corner! I can't recommend Dani highly enough."

Adam Malone, *Procurement Leader*

"Her marriage of potent commercial experience, strong yet sensitive leadership and exceptional emotional intelligence equips her perfectly to significantly enhance the careers and effectiveness of the people she mentors. Dani's positivity and empathetic approach are infectious and unquestionably gets results for those looking to grow themselves professionally and personally."

James Warren, *Rolls-Royce Motor Cars*

"Dani delivered for Defence and Security (Leadership and Management) MSc with passion, experience and credibility. In fact, her content and guest lectures have inspired me to develop Diversity as an academic line in the Defence and Security (Leadership and Management) MSc Programme."

Dr Bryan Watters OBE,
Professor and Course Director for Executive MSc in Defence Leadership, Cranfield University

"Dani Grieveson has the ability and capacity to lift and build your team, to energise it, revitalise it and to make all your people effective. Use her – it's worth it."

Zahra Pabani, *Partner, Irwin Mitchell LLP*

Printed in Great Britain
by Amazon